ALSO BY JAMES SCHUYLER

THE LETTERS OF JAMES
SCHUYLER
TO FRANK O'HARA

THE LETTERS OF JAMES SCHUYLER TO FRANK O'HARA

EDITED BY WILLIAM CORBETT
TURTLE POINT PRESS NEW YORK 2006

Request for permission to make copies of any
part of the work should be sent to:
Turtle Point Press
info@turtlepointpress.com

ISBN 978-1-885586-48-3 LCCN 2005926848

CONTENTS

INTRODUCTION

James Schuyler encountered the poet Frank O'Hara in 1951 in the little magazine *Accent*. Schuyler had three stories in the issue, and O'Hara "The Three-Penny Opera," a poem that made a strong impression on Schuyler. When Schuyler remarked on it in a phone conversation to his Buffalo friend and soon-to-be director of the Tibor de Nagy Gallery, John Bernard Myers, Myers replied, "Why, my dear, he's here in the room." The two men did not actually meet until several months later, at the party after Larry Rivers's October 1 opening at Tibor de Nagy. O'Hara introduced himself, immediately making a point about the news that André Gide's wife had burned all his letters to her: "I never liked Gide, but I didn't realize he was a complete shit." Thus began a friendship through which, in Schuyler's words to O'Hara biographer Brad Gooch, "We talked a long time, or rather, as was often the case, he talked and I listened."

At the time O'Hara lived in a sixth-floor walk-up at 326 East 49th Street with his former Harvard roommate, Hal Fondren. When Fondren moved out, O'Hara stayed on alone in the $31-a-month apartment before Schuyler joined him in the summer of 1952. The apartment, in what was then a working-class neighborhood, was within walking distance of the Museum of Modern Art, where O'Hara worked, and the Periscope-Holliday Bookstore on 54th Street, where Schuyler worked. It was also a short walk to City Center and the ballet, which both Schuyler and O'Hara loved. Schuyler shared the apartment on and off with O'Hara—with John Ashbery frequently camping out in it—until O'Hara moved downtown in 1957.

Beginning in January 1954, when O'Hara was in Southampton, Long Island, at Larry Rivers's house, Schuyler and O'Hara spent enough time apart that they corresponded. Schuyler's letters to O'Hara are sweeter in tone than any others he wrote. The easy intimacy of their friendship is evident at once and continues through Schuyler's eager "I can't wait to hear *all*" in his last letter to O'Hara, dated September 5, 1958. These men clearly liked each other a great deal; their senses of humor were in sync, and they moved in the same world of musicians, painters, and poets. Yet after 1957 they drifted apart. There was no sudden rupture, as O'Hara had with other close friends. Instead, their lives simply went in different directions. O'Hara's was on the ascent, while Schuyler's, following a severe nervous breakdown in March 1961, took him out of Manhattan to live with Fairfield Porter's family in Southampton and Maine.

We will learn more about their friendship when Nathan

Kernan's biography of Schuyler appears, but it may be that O'Hara found Schuyler's mental problems, and their transformative and prolonged nature, difficult to tolerate. When Schuyler asked to return to 49th Street in 1956 after his breakup with pianist Arthur Gold, O'Hara welcomed him back. But O'Hara's friend Joe LeSueur had moved in, which meant LeSueur and O'Hara then had to share O'Hara's bed. Privacy in the spacious apartment—whose only sink, and hence the only place to shave, was in the kitchen—became a problem. So did housekeeping, in what was already known to their friends as "Squalid Manor." Schuyler, troubled by his breakup with Gold, had a series of anxiety attacks that left him a depressed and heavy presence in the apartment. And an irksomely untidy one too. In *Digressions on Some Poems by Frank O'Hara* LeSueur recalls that Schuyler drank buttermilk constantly, scattering empty encrusted glasses throughout the apartment. LeSueur saw that the arrangement wasn't working. When he told O'Hara he was moving out O'Hara replied, "Don't leave me." They soon moved to the second of the four apartments they shared.

In these letters to O'Hara, the grip of illness that periodically and painfully seized hold of Schuyler is absent. These are the letters of a happy young man, of one good friend to another, avid to share *all*. They loved books, movies—

all sorts of movies—painting, music, ballet, and gossip. As writers they were at the start of their careers—not that they seemed to think of themselves as having embarked on anything so grand as *careers*.

From our vantage point we can see that Schuyler and O'Hara shared something more. Both men had begun with interests that they were turning away from. O'Hara had wanted to be a pianist, and he had hoped to teach and compose. Before entering Harvard he had considered the New England Conservatory, Eastman School in Rochester, New York, and Philadelphia's Curtis Institute. Harvard satisfied O'Hara's parents, and its music department, chaired by composer Walter Piston, appealed to O'Hara. However, in college and then in graduate school at the University of Michigan at Ann Arbor, O'Hara became a poet.

Schuyler had wanted to write short stories modeled on those that appeared in *The New Yorker*. It was a vague notion that stayed with him after he flunked out of Bethany College, served in the navy during World War II, and spent a few years in Italy, where he moved in W. H. Auden's circle. In the pages of *Accent* Schuyler may have recognized how much more advanced O'Hara was than he. In the months that followed, several of which were spent in Bloomingdale Hospital in White Plains, New York, after a breakdown, Schuyler, inspired by O'Hara's poetry, began to write poems. He soon finished his first published poem, "Salute."

During their time at 49th Street Schuyler, who was writing his novel *Alfred and Guinevere*, and O'Hara showed each other their work in a comradely way. It was the opposite of today's workshop professionalism. The poems and prose they wrote were to be not studied but enjoyed and admired. This casual confident approach signaled a determination not to be driven by literary aspirations. The work came first. Since they lived in a world of art, music, and writing, the rest would follow naturally. The freedom they gave each other to do exactly as they pleased, replete in these letters, must have been exhilarating.

THE LETTERS OF JAMES
SCHUYLER
TO FRANK O'HARA

Pearl Without Price,

First the worst: your five dollar check bounced. *N'importe.* I made it good, and you can pay me back when . . . the primroses come back to 49th Street.

Everybody is sick. The boys [Arthur Gold and Robert Fizdale][1] from air travel, me with a bug in the gut that keeps me lolling in the can. And the streets are swimming in swill, like the opening of *Bleak House*.

Arthur thumbs-downed the apt. on 21st Street, and we're going to live in the Chelsea![2] My favorite hotel; and I've always dreamt of living in a hotel, with its parade of maids bringing fresh linens, and a switchboard to call you

1. Arthur Gold (1917–1990) and Robert Fizdale (1920–1995) met at Manhattan's Juilliard School in 1944 and formed their piano duo, Gold and Fizdale. In the summer of 1953 Gold and Schuyler became lovers, a relationship that lasted three years. Gold and Fizdale performed an extensive two-piano repertory until their retirement in 1982. They also co-authored biographies of Misia Sert and Sarah Bernhardt.

2. Hotel Chelsea, 222 West 23rd Street in Manhattan. In 1979 Schuyler's friends Ruth Kligman and Anne Dunn moved him into Room 625 of the hotel, where he spent the rest of his life. Today a plaque affixed to the front of the Chelsea commemorates Schuyler's residence there.

in the morning. The apt. will be quite nice with a big, big room for the pianos & sitting, and a good-sized one (completely cut off from the piano practice) for sleeping and me. I know I'll like it.

What are you writing? What are Larry [Rivers] and Fairfield [Porter] painting?[3] What are you painting? What are they writing?

Arthur & I saw *In the Summer House*[4] Wednesday night —more laughter & tears, and no diminution of satisfaction.

I told John to give me the five to send or to send it himself, and he said you want to go to the opening (Feb. 2) of *Nutcracker* with him, and he's going to buy your ticket out of the five. So you can leave it so, or write him different.

The enclosed is a pin-money present for my Sweet Singer from County Cork. Spend it in good health.

My love to Larry and Fairfield and their respective households.

Remember me to our mother the sea.

Toujours ton bête,

Jimmy

3. O'Hara is in Southampton, New York, living with painter Larry Rivers (1923–2002) and often visiting Fairfield Porter (1907–1975).

4. Play by Jane Bowles (1917–1973), which had opened on Broadway in 1953.

Sweets,

I'm "having" Mildred today. I mean to say, I'm letting her "do" the apartment. But I left her a note to call me and I'll tell her to skip this next Monday, and come the one after, when you'll be back: right?

And I'm forwarding two decidedly dull looking letters, all the mail there's been except for an announcement of Leatrice Rose's show at Hansa[5] and a card saying last Saturday was Café Night at the Club.[6]

Jane [Freilicher] picked up a frying pan at Joe's [Hazan][7] this morning, unaware that the electric had been on under it for twenty-four hours, and burned her hand, but not, she says, too badly. When I talked to her she was painting with a greasy rag wrapped around it, something like the old age of Renoir.

5. Hansa Gallery (1952–1959) on 10th Street, named after painter and teacher Hans Hofmann.

6. A group of downtown artists who sponsored lectures, readings, panel shows, concerts, and dances.

7. Jane Freilicher (b. 1924), painter. Close friend of O'Hara and Schuyler and, during this period, their muse. Joe Hazan, painter and husband of Jane Freilicher.

Thank you for your dear note, dear. My love to Larry and Fairfield, and tell Berdie *I* asked after *her*.[8] I trust these nippy days you've added a sealskin coat to your otherwise perfect posing outfit. I await with interest Southampton's new lubricious masterworks.

Don't dare to come home with less than a long novella.

Toujours ton,

Jimmy

PS I trust your love for me isn't something that could be drained off in letters—!

HOTEL CHELSEA

1/21

Bright bauble,

When is who going to call who where? Is it *this* Sat. you're coming in? *I'll* be at the Chelsea, Ch 3-3700, ext. 129.

---

8. Bertha "Berdie" Berger, Larry Rivers's mother-in-law, kept house for Rivers and was beloved by many of Rivers's friends, including O'Hara. His sonnet to her, "Mrs. Bertha Berger," begins, "Her life is beautiful, and free from hate." She died in 1958. In *Larry Rivers: A Memoir* O'Hara wrote of her that she "held together a Bohemian household of such staggering complexity that it would have driven a less great woman mad."

4

A[rthur] sends you his love. He has intestinal 'flu, nonetheless, he must leave tomorrow for a week.

"Opus 34"[9] left me feeling rather *je m'en fiche*. John [Ashbery][10] says Jane liked it, he himself was unable to formulate an opinion. It seemed to me rather a joke at the expense of J[erome] Robbins'[11] age of anxieties.

The temperature seems to be dropping a degree a second. What can it mean?

Bring your new poems. xxxx

xxxx

Jimmy

Dear Kitten,

A word or two to say I got your letter, and while it's a joy to hear from you, I'm sorry the world weighs so heavily.

9. Ballet by George Balanchine to music by Arnold Schoenberg.

10. John Ashbery (b. 1927), poet, art critic, and playwright who stayed at East 49th when he was in town.

11. Jerome Robbins (1918–1998), dancer and choreographer of ballets and Broadway musicals. In 1950 the New York City Ballet premiered his ballet *The Age of Anxiety* with music by Leonard Bernstein. The ballet's title came from W. H. Auden's "Baroque Eclogue," *The Age of Anxiety*.

Your family sitch. seems to demand of you a Zen-like repose. I think the town & country living idea sounds ideal: now you must undertake some extended literary task—but you know how hipped I am on the big Push, & little by little.

I haven't been by the apartment since last week, since I had a long weekend off, & don't know if there's mail for you —I'll try to get by this evening. John has had my keys, and made use of them. He's in the dumps and so is Jane, who has a cold.

I'm not in the dumps and I don't have a cold, so I suppose I ought to be feeling nervous. But what the hell—

My love to Larry & all, and a smacking big kiss for you.

J.

HOTEL CHELSEA

MARCH 15

My wounded wood dove,

I hope this finds you in a deck chair, bundled up in tartans, healing yourself in the revivifying salt air. *No* posing naked in draughty studios: doctor's orders.[12]

Here is the 5, and here is the deposit receipt. So Maureen

---

12. O'Hara had posed in the nude for Rivers's portrait after Géricault; the image would be turned down for the cover of his *Collected Poems* but used as the cover of his *Selected*.

[O'Hara][13] will have the benefit of an education. Perhaps you ought to interest her in going on the stage.

I feel quite ghastly today: we gave a big cocktail party yesterday, and had a sneak-preview of Jane's show for significant New Yorkers. Jane's paintings looked "marvie" in the apartment, and I think some of the people really took to them. But how can you ever tell? Needless to say, quite a deal of whiskey got under the hosts' belts. I think this evening a shady movie-house will suit.

John was blue at lunch today (for a change), and after he got through the saga of Phil [O'Hara],[14] he looked distant and said, "Sometimes I wish the Raggle-Taggle gypsies would come and take me away."

Give Larry my love and tell Berdie how pleased I am that she likes that poem of mine—and remember me to the boys and to Augusta.[15] I attend your return, and hope I'll be able to wander around saying—"Look at Frank: he has *roses* in his cheeks."

Love,

Jimmy

13. Maureen (O'Hara) Granville-Smith, the youngest of three O'Hara children and the executor of her brother Frank's estate.

14. O'Hara's younger brother, Philip, visiting from basic training at Fort Bragg.

15. Augusta Berger, wife of Larry Rivers.

PS George Davis says Saturday at the *3 Penny* is sold out—so we'll try the next Wednesday (the 24th)[16] & will you be in town that night?

Tête d'or,

If you're "in" your play, I think it would be silly to stay over Wednesday night just to see old *3 Penny*. Don't do it. It will still be going when you come back for next month's reviews,[17] and that will be time enough.

So many people have asked after you, all have expressed horror of the event, concern for you, and delight at your release from the hospital and hair-breadth 'scape.[18] Virgil T[homson] is one who comes to mind, and another is Ben Weber.[19] He wants to see you before he leaves for Rome:

16. Bertolt Brecht's *Threepenny Opera*, starring Lotte Lenya.

17. O'Hara came into Manhattan to do reviews for *Art News*.

18. A mugger had stopped O'Hara in the foyer of his apartment building and, when O'Hara turned away from him, shot him in the buttocks.

19. Ben Weber (1916–1979), composer. O'Hara's essay "About Ben Weber" appeared in *Standing Still and Walking in New York*, edited by Donald Allen and published by Gray Fox in 1975.

around, I think it is, the 29th. Why don't you call him Tuesday? And he'll be at the concert.

I can't think of anything newsworthy—I'm having lunch in a few minutes with Bernie Oshei, and John Myers just left: sounds like the Social Notes in the *East Aurora Advertiser*.[20]

I've been working on a sort of a thing but if I don't see any large, or any, design in it, I don't much care. As long as a fellow keeps up his plain-sewing and hem-stitching there's bound to be something in his hope chest some day— I always say.

It's a frisky St. Patrick's Day. The sun is radiant and the wind chill. I hope you're about to take a long stroll on the tan strand (wi', of course, your gold hems i' your hair).

I'll be glad when Tuesday next is past. Goodness, I hope people will *like* the piece: you, in particular. I really think you will. It is, at any rate, a relief to feel it will be done as well as possible: so different from anticipating *P[resenting] Jane*

20. Bernard Oshei (b. 1922) was Schuyler's closest friend during adolescence. There are numerous references to their friendship in *The Morning of the Poem*. Schuyler met John Bernard Myers (1914–1987) while he was in high school and Myers worked at a Buffalo, New York, bookstore. Myers was the first director of the Tibor de Nagy Gallery and a major animator of the New York painter and poet scene from the early 1950s until his death.

9

last year![21] I think you may end by proposing to Gloria Davis: such a looker.[22] They do a have a way of making us white folks seem just under-done.

My best to *ton méages* and my best love to you.

xxx

Jimmy

Dear Boy,

Here I am, on the humid ocean, eating English cooking and hating it, and drinking English gin and loving it.

Arthur & I seldom take our faces out of a Berlitz German book—and when I do, it's to put mine into a book on Austria, or else into my pillow.

---

21. Play by Schuyler. Jane is Jane Freilicher. Schuyler wrote the play in the spring of 1952, and that summer John LaTouche filmed scenes from it at a rented house in East Hampton. In February 1953 John Bernard Myers's and Herbert Machiz's Artists' Theatre produced the play at the Theatre de Lys in Greenwich Village.

22. Gloria Davis was one of four singers in the original cast of Paul Bowles's *A Picnic Cantata* with words by Schuyler.

The Tourist Class is entirely a Nest of Ninnies, which suits their laureate very well.[23]

The sailing was uneventfully thrilling—my dear, the only way to see Manhattan's foot is as it grows small and fades and turns into the tiniest idea.

It's 12 noon, and Arthur just got up, so it's back to "*Was ist das?*" and "*Was tun sie?*" for me.

I'll write a real letter when I'm in a real place. I adore you and am thine,

Love,

Jimmy

(I'm getting around the fact that I don't know if there are 31 days in August)

Fair slender bough,

Greetings from the Adriatic Pearl. It's marvelous here, I'm delighted to be here, and don't want to hear another

23. Schuyler and John Ashbery collaborated on the novel *A Nest of Ninnies* beginning in 1952. They finished it in 1968, and it was published the following year by Dutton.

word about Austria. All that's lacking is yourself, tripping between the pigeons and the cats.

I'm really so foolishly pleased with such vast extents of Venetian art that it's falling into a bottomless pit of delight. I can't tell you how my legs ached last week or, what's more remarkable, how little I minded. The high aesthetic life doesn't, alas, make for lively letters . . .

How did the movie scripts turn out? What happened in Southampton? Besides painting, swimming and dancing. What are you working on, what have you written and have you worked up your play? And I want to hear all about John Myers; will there be an A's [Artists'] Theatre this year? Has anyone killed Herbert [Machiz][24] yet? Write me everything.

I've been reading an entertaining book I found in the apartment, Clarendon's *History of the Rebellion*. It's sort of a cross between Jane Austen and Walton's *Lives*, and comes in five dictionary-sized volumes, so it's quite a task to haul one into bed, and then quite hard to get it off the bed again. I'd forgotten though what an appetite I can have for something other than novels and verse. And plays.

24. Herbert Machiz (1923–1976), director of the Artists' Theatre and lover of John Myers.

I started to write a little play, and dropped it and went back to my insufferable novel.[25] It would be just too boring not to finish it, and besides, once I have finished it, I'll be free to entangle myself in something else.

The intent of this is to lure you into writing me, and if you write me a lovely letter, somewhere between laughter and tears, I promise I'll do better by you next time. I miss you and send you a shower of kisses.

Love,
Jimmy

[Handwritten note from Arthur Gold]

Dear Frank, Do you know what I said to J. after our first day in Venice? Well, I said. Do you know who would like Venice of all the people we know?

J.—Who?

Me—Frank.

J.—Why?

Me—Because it's all water surrounded by small land lagoons.

25. Schuyler's novel *Alfred and Guinevere*, published by Harcourt Brace in 1958.

And you would and should write and tell us about all the beauties in the New World—

Love

Venice Gold

AMERICAN EXPRESS

VENICE, ITALY

SEPT. 28, 1954

Dear Frank,

The enclosed limp lines (which I shall bundle into the envelope like so much yesterday's salad) were meant to celebrate your return to 49th Street. Oh dear, they're so well meant, and so unmendable to me. I'm discouragingly (or do I mean, discouragedly?) aware that the first line sounds as though the next should be: "can face the world full square," but have no idea of how to mend it. I thought of making it "... who talks with his head up ..." but that seems too suggestive of, "The boy who talks with his head." Perhaps you could suggest something; anyway, for now, I send it as it issued from the old mattress stuffer's hand, lumpy and unquilted.

The last line of the second stanza was supposed to mean, simply, that when wild things happen to us, we behave like ourselves. Though I seem to have taken an odd route to say it.

No new news. Bobby [Fizdale] got your letter, and we all grow restive with the second report on the ballet. What a fiend that Balanchine is, imagine going to Los Angeles for the summer and coming back with two new masterpieces.[26]

Stanley Barrows has been here, and told me about some literary fellowship at Leland Stanford that sounds profitable. I think you have to spend some time there, but not all, and there's quite a sum attached. I suppose one could just write to Leland S's English department and ask—I don't know.

Have you found a part-time job? What's your impression of the T[ibor] de N[agy] group show? And what's the gallery's address? I want to send John [Bernard Myers] a card.

Here comes a flight of kisses from me:

your,

Jimmy

> *The boy who walks with his head up*
> *and speaks in flights, and dives*
> *(so I fear to follow, or fear for him)*
> *into the phosphor falling hurricane,*

26. George Balanchine (1904–1983), Russian-born choreographer, was a founder and artistic director of the New York City Ballet.

who, when creeks flow swollen after rain
and gold light turns pink on limbs
(so I grow envious, and wish to follow), swims

the boy who met a terror on the stair
face to face, and turned,
and didn't wait to reason (as I might),
but plunged and stopped a bullet in its flight
where it hurt least and caused least damage,
who feels the weather in his wound, has learned
how our wild moments are our own,

the boy I mean I see in rooms I know
from which the well-loved phone is gone,
with his head full of words, go
and shut the gas and fetch a perking pot
to the stuffed desk at which he writes,
the boy who turns and sees from his window
a river with gulls diving in long flights.

AMERICAN EXPRESS

ROME, ITALY

OCT. 8, 1954

Dear Frank,

I never like to write letters after 6 in the evening (it's just 6)—I'm so afraid I may describe the sunset, or mention my aspirations—but I've got to send thanks, on the day I got it, for your greatest of letters. Dear boy, I'm so enchanted by your excursion. Like Pushkin, you must turn to prose— something about the length of Pique Dame, in the style of Svevo?[27] But after your letter, you are the American Svevo. But you must write a story of our friends, and their by you so clearly seen ways: a few coolly sketched scenes at the beach, perhaps, coiling into something snappy in a road-house, with a hurricane for epilogue?

My past week has been very men in white, since Arthur got terribly sick with bronchitis. He's over it now, with the help of American wonder drugs and a Venetian doc who, for reasons not clear, spends three months a year in New York, where he knows a lot of gangsters who take him to the

27. Italo Svevo (1861–1928), pseudonym of Italian novelist Ettore Schmitz, best known for his novel *Confessions of Zeno*.

Latin Quarter. I helped the time pass by reading *Dombey and Son* aloud, which at first I loved and then got to hate, and then *Injury and Insult*,[28] the title of the first translation of *I*'d & *I*'d. Have you ever read it? It's full of the most exhilarating self-preoccupation, and depressing in that thorough exhausting way that's such a relief to the nerves. When reading the big speeches aloud, I model myself on your great Chekhov performances.[29] Works like a charm.

The most intoxicating thing has happened to the weather here. At the beginning of the week, the sun went into hiding for a couple of days, and when it came back, its light had turned as gold as a grape. It's marvelous to have gotten to know Venice well, and then have it turn in a day into something so much more beautiful—all the hard whites have turned to cream and roses, and the dry stucco colors have gotten as rich as autumn leaves. How I wish you were here—they say it happens again in the spring, and I know it will next October—ought we to begin to plan?

I'm already beginning to worry about how I'll work, the next two months. Oh dear, I'm sure Trollope had the right

28. *The Insulted and Injured*, a novel by Fyodor Dostoyevsky.

29. O'Hara, Schuyler, Gold, and Fizdale read Chekhov aloud in a house the pianists rented at Snedens Landing, New York, in the summer of 1953.

idea, whatever it was. But will I have something to show you? Yes, I think I must, even if it's mere Raspings from an Old Loaf.

You still don't tell what five poems *Poetry* took. So tell.

Isn't it ghastly that I didn't send anything to Richard Miller?[30] I meant to, but I forgot in the whirl of leaving. Phooey. I suppose I should write him a graceful note, and make it clear that it wasn't on purpose, just weak witted-ness. (I suppose there are lots more t's in that.)

But speaking of Richard: in ways too involved to unroll, I have the enclosed (something to do with paying for a book), and as I can't cash it here, why don't you have it, on what all our favorite museums dote to call extended loan? I know you can use it, and I'm afraid all it will do here is turn from a good check to a bad check.

Now I have to go make a phone call, and find out what time the local vaudeville starts: there's a magician tonight. Zowie.

I had a card from Janice [Koch] in Geneva, and Chester

30. In 1961 Richard Miller's Tiber Press published Schuyler's *Salute* with prints by Grace Hartigan, Frank O'Hara's *Odes* with prints by Michael Goldberg, *Permanently* by Kenneth Koch with prints by Alfred Leslie, and John Ashbery's *The Poems* with prints by Joan Mitchell.

[Kallman] in Calabria, and shortly I'll be seeing [William] Weaver in Rome.[31] Italy's foreign, but not too.

Write me soon. A thousand thanks again for your heavenly letter. The boys, who are up to their elbows in Debussy, send their love.

Love,
Jimmy

Dear Frank,

"What props't, thou asks'ts . . ."? Why the picture you sent me, of course, darling boy. What a sweet thought, what heaven to have it.

I was so moved by the two Whitman poems I went straight to the Lion Bookshop to get myself a *Leaves* to read

31. Janice Koch (1931–1981) was the wife of Kenneth Koch and a close friend of Schuyler's. Chester Kallman (1921–1975), a poet, was W. H. Auden's lover and a friend of Schuyler's from the early 1940s. William Weaver (b. 1923) was a writer and translator residing in Rome.

in the country; which of course they didn't have. Beastly English dykes (who run the shop that is). So I got a selected Matthew Arnold (Why?), *Twelfth Night* & the *Sonnets* (here's a sortes virgiliana for you:

"........ and think of nought

save where you were, how happy you make those.")
and Houghton's *Life & Letters of Keats*. Now I wish I'd gotten *Oblomov* and a big Shelley. Oh well.

Bill [Weaver] told me he wrote you a long letter, which seems somewhat to take the wind out of my sails. I trust you detected my feelings between the lines of his description of that vilest of movies he dragooned me into seeing! The dear boy. He's been helpfulness itself, and made me feel Rome's own guest.

I'm out of my mind for the place I think I'll live. I'm going there on Monday, at the latest.

The last few days, I've seen lots of Jimmy Throneberg, and recommend him to your tender care. I think Joe [Le-Sueur] is very lucky.[32] How is Gianni [Bates] taking it?[33] I gather he took it quite badly last summer—but it seemed

32. Joe LeSueur (1924–2001), writer and Frank O'Hara's roommate from 1955 to 1965.

33. Gianni Bates, set designer, photographer, and a lover of Joe LeSueur's. O'Hara wrote a poem to him, "To Gianni Bates."

like such a doomed affair last winter. But Jimmy T *is* cute and funny and dry. I wonder what his writing is like?

Please show the "Home Book" to Richard [Miller]. I don't know what copy is there—in most, I've cut bits here and there. But show it to him, and if you think it needs editing, let me know. Would you—angel of men—read through it for typing mistakes? I think there are a lot.

Yesterday Jimmy T and I went to the Borghese Gallery (and got there too late to get in), and coming back through the pines, who should we find sitting on a toad stool, but toad of toad hollow himself, Harold Norse.[34] He's giving English lessons here (it rather chilled me in Venice, to find him sitting outside the Fenice, writing his diary). But after we had exchanged words and gone on, I suddenly remembered what Harold once said about Joe not being for street wear, and told it to Jimmy. My dear, I thought there'd be blood in the Borghese Gardens then. But he contented himself with pointing out what a shame it is so many Italians are going to end speaking English with a little swishy accent . . .

But the future holds better things than Harold. Al Kresch[35] is due this weekend, on a week's visit. What fun.

34. Harold Norse (b. 1916), poet and memoirist.
35. Al Kresch (b. 1923), painter.

And the Kochs are in the offing. Oh baby, why aren't you here to help me spike the punch?

I'm madly depressed today, and writing to you is the only cheerful thing I can think of doing. I've been feeling much less gifted than Harold Norse, and letters I look for don't come, and I feel I ought to have gone to the country today, but feel terribly nervous about getting to work, and imagine that all that will come out of my typewriter is a long sob and a hiccup. And a very very very silly Italian boy has decided my spell is fatal, and follows me around, and makes preferred haunts unhauntable, singing American love songs with the words all jumbled up. But now I feel better.

And, feeling better and thinking of you, go off to pick up Jimmy T and eat boiled chicken with him at Bill's.

Is Chester [Kallman] back and have you seen him? Write me unceasingly: surely the season is far enough advanced for the dirt to have begun to fly? Give my love to everyone in New York named John, no matter how it's spelled. And to Jane, Fairfield and Hal [Fondren]. But keep the biggest share for yourself.

Love,
Jimmy

Dear Frank,

Just a note to tell you that I'm taking your note to the local tapestry works, where I'm going to have it copied in Parker blue on Sphinx typing paper, gray, wall-size. And my idea of wall-size is the northern flank of the UN Building. You're cute, that's what you are.

Anguillara didn't work out for beans, so I'm established in a somewhat meager, but pleasant, little hotel in Rome. My days are full, fair and fine, but my evenings barren of any sort of intercourse. I've become a moviegoer again, if not a bug or fan; it's like being an opium addict without getting any lift. Let's see, I've seen: *Witness to Murder, Mogambo, Ulisee* (I saw it in Italian, so that's what I call it), de Sica's dud, *Stazione Termini, On the Waterfront, From Here to . . .* and a couple of Italian ones I won't go into. Not to put a fine point on it, I thought them all hell; though many featured nice-lookers caught looking their best. Tonight it's a toss-up between Danny Kaye, dubbed, or Gérard Philippe, not dubbed. Maybe I'll just duck over to the forum and worship a heathen idol instead.

If you don't tell me what poems you have in *Poetry*, I'll . . . I don't know what I'll do. Gnash my teeth, perhaps.

Al K[resch] was here, and having so much fun. He couldn't sit down without drawing, and he vanished one morning into the Vatican before 9, and had a fit when they told him at 2 they were closing. I can't spend ten minutes there without thinking how far I am from the nearest comfortable café. But now he's back in Munich. And Bill [Weaver] is in Vienna, as are the boys. (Do, if you haven't, write Bill: it seemed as though every time we went to Amer. Exp. together, I got a letter from you. Or so it seemed to him! You know how rejectable our young folk are nowadays.)

This is just a silly Sunday evening note, brought on by your note, which touched me so.

Love,

Jimmy

ps Have you met, and what do you think of J. Throne-berg?

ps Write me c/o Amer. Exp. Piazza di Spagna, Rome & mark "hold."

Dear Frank,

From the slums of downtown Rome I've moved, for a brief stay, to one of the august seven hills (which, escapes me at the moment—the nice one). I like it. As little J[ohn] A[shbery] said when he got drunk at Lincoln Kirsten's housewarming, "I love your new house and your new apartment."

And speaking of whom, he wrote me from Sodus that you're working mornings for [Cecil] Beaton.[36] Praise Venus for part-time labor: is it part-time enough? Remunerated enough? Is he entertaining? Is he nice? I hope the answer to all is yes.

The boys have been here three days, and that's fun. I was really getting quite very bored; the evenings are such a drag.

36. Cecil Beaton (1904–1980), British photographer, set designer, and diarist. In November and December 1954 O'Hara worked mornings as his secretary.

It's all very well at the beach in a cottage, with the lapse of the waves, or in the mountains in a cabin, with the snapping pine knots and the whining of the beasts (such as bears, mountain lions, and big mean jack rabbits), but in a city, continued solitude begins to make me feel like little Nellie nose-to-the-pane, watching the rich child's burf-day party. But with *tutta Roma* at my feet, I feel quite King for a Day-ish.

There go the bells: sundown and vespers. I wonder what the pope is thinking? And Lucky Luciano, way down there in Naples, what's he thinking?[37]

And what do you think of this?: May I come live with you again? In February and March (and perhaps more)? Bobby has his place, but Arthur and I don't. As soon as we get back —the first week of February, the first day or so, in fact—he goes off on a tour, and will be away most of two months. I don't want to live at Arthur Weinstein's[38] (not that I've had my arm twisted to do it: let's face it, I like him fine, but left to ourselves, we are not a "natural"). Oh well this is dumb,

37. Charles "Lucky" Luciano (1897–1962), New York gangster deported to his native Naples. Luciano was a founder of Murder Incorporated.

38. Arthur Weinstein, interior decorator.

there's nothing to explain that isn't obvious: I'd rather live at home with you on 49th Street, than alone in some dump. So write me it can be! By then, though you may have taken a sloe-eyed god to your bosom, bed and board? (For heaven sakes, don't change the sheets on my bed; they were quite fresh when I left. . . .)

I confess that my second thought, after thinking of writing you this, was, "Frank and I never did really give that little at-home party. . ."

Oh dear, autumn sadness is looking in the window, in the shape of black firs and deep blue sky. Cocktail time, and I know for a certain fact, there's no gin in the house, which seems a disgrace, when the best English sort costs less than $3 here. Should I throw away my clothes when I come home, and just bring gin?

This seems an excessively dumb letter; I did work hard today, but that's no excuse.

Forgive me, love me, and write me an outline of your plans as of ten weeks from now (ten weeks seems, sounds, so much sooner than "next February." Where is time taking us, do you suppose?)

Bobby said he had a darling letter from you. The boys aren't here, but I'll send their love anyway, with simple confidence.

Has Hal [Fondren] a job? (If he hasn't, don't tell him I

asked! For if he hasn't, he must really be quite depressed about it by now.)

My address remains American Express and so on.

Love,

Jimmy

Dear Vladimir,

I received your Dawn of Civilization letter the way the Babylonians greeted Sohrab when he descended from Mount Rustum with the clay plates incised with Gilgamesh. Epics of thanks, adored diverting one.

Your letter (and one from Fairfield, which I also got yesterday) was the first I knew that I'd come out in *Partisan Review*. Whee. I was so gloomily certain they were going to put it in that *Are These Our Children?* semi-annual pocket reader they do; and, as you said, it's so nice to see one's own in that distinctive Parisian type-face.

Today I got a check from them for 16.50. Or maybe it was 15.60. That will pay for my postage for the next month, at least.

I wish you had sent me *Poetry*; I have dim hopes of find-

29

ing it in this hick burg. But if you didn't, remember that I enjoined you to buy and keep a copy for me. I love to think of us together on the stands (you know, like when Marlon's on *Time* and Monty's on *Life*?).

The boys played the Poulenc with the Santa Cecilia (whose day it was yesterday) and got raves from audience and critics—the incomparable couple, one reviewer called them. The concerto came after a rather flat-footed Vivaldi piece and some Dallapiccola mood-music, and sounded, so placed (and played: it's a heavenly orchestra), more than ever like Constance Mozart's masterpiece. Then Friday a recital here, on which the things that you haven't heard them play (I don't think you have) will be *Scaramouche* and the Brahms' *Haydn Variations*. The boys' concerts have caused some high-class wining and dining: the night before last, a banker from Baltimore assured me that he thought writing poems must be much more difficult than banking; and last night a lady from L.A. asked me, "Well, are you just writing a novel or are you—if you'll excuse my expression— trying to prove something?" All either of them got from me was my Mona Lisa laugh. And I met Respighi's widow and Casella's widow. Italy has changed not much since the days of the Princess Zoubaroff.[39]

39. Ronald Firbank's play, *The Princess Zoubaroff, a Comedy*.

A word in your nacre ear: I don't think I have to bring you and Arthur together, but rather convince you of how sincerely fond of you Arthur is, how much he admires your talent and how much it delights him to be with you. He is also, though, as sensitive to tension and rejection—real, imagined, accidental or apparent—as you or I. I say that because I think the feeling that makes you suggest a bringing together affects him as much as the reverse would you (and no more).

I'm glad you sent the deK's [de Koonings'] addresses, for I wanted them. Bill's room was the best thing at the Biennale,[40] along with the Courbets (which weren't a "great" selection, though there was many a stunner). It was strange seeing them out of New York City, they looked so much "quieter" than I would have expected; they seemed to make no extra theatrical bid, beyond that of denseness and quality, in the way I imagine [Jackson] Pollock and [Mark] Rothko did. I guess what I mean is that what struck me was the way his pictures *don't* depend on manner; it didn't seem like two rooms of de Koonings but two rooms of paintings.

I saw Elliot Stein here for a split minute, who asked me to convey his esteem to you, Ashes, et al.

My dear, I'm depositing your letter in a vault, so that if

40. The XXVII Venice Biennale, de Kooning's second.

you are murdered in a waterfront hotel, the police will know who to arrest. Ted Gorey has not *thought* since 1948 that you would be stabbed, he's simply been planning to kill you.[41] Why do you think he wears that Laird Craiger (Creger?) beard?[42] And reads those flocks of unreadable detective stories? Because he thinks he's Alpha and Omega come to save the world from beauty's snare: and you, you see, are too beautiful! So swear you'll never ever see him unless accompanied by at least three stout friends.

Or to put it another way, I despise the inimitable Teddles. He hasn't enough brains to animate a Kewpie doll or enough talent to make a good joke. I also feel sorry for him, because he's frustrated, unhappy, he lives vicariously, and it makes him sadistic.

Turning to pleasanter thoughts: I never felt, rubbed, touched, brushed up against, bumped into, caressed, dallied with, sucked or was fucked by, JT's cock: I also never saw it pendant above a toilet bowl, aimed at a urinal, raise its head and take a sip from his wine glass or go sliding along

41. Edward Gorey (1925–2000), book designer, artist, and writer. Gorey had been O'Hara's Harvard roommate.

42. Laird Cregar (1916–1945), actor who played Jack the Ripper in *The Lodger*.

32

the floor, rubbing its back on the chair legs. So, in re: its size, I refer you to JleS [Joe LeSueur]. Sorry!

Actually, I liked him like you like a friend; but since you say you find him "presentable," I take it that that might mystify you.

So JAbery saw my letter to Jane [Freilicher], huh. Well well. I didn't think I said anything bitchy, just that you had caught him in characteristic attitudes, as indeed you had everyone who was on the excursion. But mercy me, if you think it will do any good, of course I'll assure him that you told me he took you and Hal to the theatre!

Poor dear Bill Weaver has jaundice in Vienna, so far from his home away from home. He wrote John Becker that it was not a serious case, but, I seem to recall that when Bill Rose had it here, he first had a mild attack, and then a very serious one. Anyway, Bill seems to think he'll be back in Rome by Dec. 1 or so—all the same, if you whisked him a note, it might reach him there: Pension Alt Wein, Spiegelgasse 6, Wein I, Austria. He's in a hospital, but J Becker, fearing his children might catch it, burned the letter! Tell JA and Hal to send him a word of cheer, too. It is soul-trying to be sick and companionless in a far place. (I wonder how many orderlies he's seduced by now? In Venice, he grabbed at, and got, the bearer of his morning coffee tray . . .)

So far I wrote yesterday, when the boys came in and we all went out to dinner in the Pecci-Blunt palace and then to the Milan train, where, this minute, the boys are playing. Someday you must teach me how to talk to strangers—I feel such a lump. My conversation encounter last night went something like this: a Mme de Beaumont: "Nowadays, so few young people seem interested in maintaining their beautiful homes, don't you find?" Me (thinking of my own young people): "Maybe it costs too much money." Mme de B: "No no no I don't mean that . . ." as I might have deduced from the beads on her fingers and the rings in her ears. Ho hum. Anyway, and besides, it's fun to see the insides of houses.

Yes, I do want to finish my novel before I come back. 1) I couldn't bear for it to keep going on and on forever, and 2) why not? And 3) even if I don't feel satisfied with it, just to finish it may give me a retrospective kind of satisfaction.

Now I'm going to go eat, and see a Venetian company in a Goldoni play, of which I'll understand powerfully little. The opera season begins here in a couple of weeks with *Forza*,[43] and this Sunday they're doing de Falla's mar-

43. Giuseppe Verdi's opera *La Forza del Destino*.

ionette opera[44] in a concert performance with Spanish singers. Goody.

I look daily for a "hurry home" answer from you to my last letter.

Bye bye for now, sweetie pie:

love,

N.N. [Nicholas Nabokov]

Jimmy

Dear Frank—

I've just done customs, & I'm sitting on the train waiting to cross the German border. Do you suppose Baden-Baden will have a ghost of the intricate days?[45] I hope so. I wouldn't want my new rhinestone bows to go for naught. I left Bill Weaver sobbing your name in Rome. But don't worry *I'll* soon be out of the woods & home.

love,

Jimmy

44. *El Retable de Maese Pedro.*

45. Refers to "those/were intricate days" in O'Hara's poem "The Three-Penny Opera."

Dear Frank,

I'm about to go meet Kenneth[46] for our first Paris reunion, which makes this seem a likely moment to use up my last sheet of this valuable paper [Jolly Hotel, Vicenza] in letting you know I'll be clasped in your arms in two weeks. We chug away on the Liberté on the 28th, and reach NY around or about Feb. 3rd. The first two days I guess I'll spend saying goodbye to my friend, A.G., for they go off to Canada right away; then on, say, the evening of the 5th, a pale but valiant Pip will stagger up the stairs.

How thrilling to think of you making 85 a week![47] My dear! I didn't know there was that much money in the world. I assume you've taken to complaining about taxes?

Since I last wrote I've been in some odd places, such as Baden-Baden, which has its own stuffy charm. But Paris is the cat's miaow, though the Seine, which is the highest it's

46. Kenneth Koch (1925–2002), poet, playwright, and Columbia University professor.

47. O'Hara had taken a job at the Museum of Modern Art as Porter McCray's Special Assistant in the International Program.

been since the floods of 1910, is about to pour into the lobby of the hotel [Hotel Quai Voltaire]. (Among the notables who have stayed here are Wagner, Baudelaire and Wilde.)

Oh dear, I just realized my little clock has stopped and Kenneth will be petulant; I can't leave him squatting at the door of the Bibliothêque Nationale. Can I? Well, I only could if it were to have a martini with you.

How's Gianni Bates by the way? Oops. That's no way to begin our beautiful new life together...

With anticipatory kisses, adorèd

love,

Jimmy

PS Here's a poem I wrote last Nov. I'm afraid it bears the old corn merchant's trademark, but I like it more than I usually like my poems.

[Enclosed: "A Head"]

Dear Frank,

Would you please put my name back on the mailbox? For I want to have my address there, here. The river is very flooded. I wonder if we will ever leave Paris. I've been seeing Kenneth, who's cute & longs to hear from you.

Love,

J

Dear Frank,

It's one of the most beautiful places I've ever been. I love it. I won't attempt to describe it, just come & come soon. Write as many of those dreadful letters as you can beforehand. I count it a *disaster* if you can't begin your vacation on August one.

I shall start looking for your play in the mail tomorrow.

We paddled to a neighboring island for lunch in a canoe, where Rosie Kennison—I think she thought I was going to be you, because she remembered having a long talk with me

38

after the Nyack concert—then she squealed at me and said, "But wasn't there a friend with you at Sneden's Landing, that's who I had the long talk with."[48] I allowed he would be with me again soon.

I cannot wait to paddle the canoe around the island with you—

Kitty [Porter] was swinging on the back screen door today, very reflectively, and said to me, "You know, I can just imagine how Frank O'Hara feels about coming here." Then she thought & said, "Can you imagine Frank here? I can."

I can too, but I'd much rather have the reality.

love,

Jimmy

PS It was fun to have a farewell drink with you on Thursday. My love to corn-hair-prairie-sky-eyed Joe [LeSueur]
                    HURRY!

PS Did you ever find that letter from East Aurora? And when *Poetry* sends back my translations let me know—

48. Rosie Kennison, sister of inventor and writer Buckminster Fuller. The Fullers had inherited Bear Island in Penobscot Bay.

Dear Frank,

I'm delighted that *Poetry* took two (a favorite joke of Bernie Oshei's and mine all through high school was, "Take a lot: take two.") though they're pigs—yes, pigs—not to have taken them all. Still, we uncircumcised poets like to get it printed now and again, and there will be at least two good poems in the issue they come out in.

I'm so entranced with it here, and want you here so much, I can't bring myself to believe that you won't somehow get away on Awg One. If you can't and you know you can't, it must be madly irritating to have me whining away. But I don't care. I'm only DOING IT FOR YOUR OWN GOOD AND OTHER SELFISH REASONS. A week here is like a month anywhere else in its breadth, depth and general spaciousness, and I feel if not like a new man then rather like an old one, who wasn't really such a bad egg now was he? On my way here on the bus I passed a movie marquee (in Fairfield, Conn.) that perfectly described how I was beginning to feel: *The Creature with the Atomic Brain*. Z-z-z-z-z-z-sputter-pop.

Don't, by the way, come by Greyhound. One does have

to change at Boston, which is a bore even if the bus makes the connection, which mine didn't. Ellen Auerbach[49] came up on a through bus (NY to Camden without change) run by a company called Trailways. It leaves NY around 7 AM and gets into Camden about 10 PM. It does mean staying over night at the Green Gables (write beforehand): and my opinion is that when you add up bus fare, meals & lodging, the only thing to do is fly. Aline Porter says the best place to fly to is Bar Harbor, which isn't far from Sunset. It's all too confusing and I leave it to Fairfield to work out, but do FLY —15 hours on buses left me chafed, constipated, cranky and with incipient piles.

Bring sweaters. Also, I was glad I brought my slicker; but it seems pointless to bring a heavy raincoat.

Has Chester [Kallman] left?

Fairfield finished a portrait of me, and I like it very much. I think it's one of his best. Pitt says she thinks there's more democracy in the way the figure and background are painted in relation to one another than in any of the portraits he showed last year, and I agree. Even I look quite sweet in a yellow Brooks shirt. I think he might call it *The*

49. Ellen Auerbach, friend of Fairfield Porter from the 1930s.

Man in the Brooks Bros. Shirt Was Nicer Than Mary Mc-Carthy Said.[50]

Well Chicken Little, the sky is falling and I must get on with what ever it is I'm working on. I've started a new novel almost every day since I've been here, and will soon be in a position to publish a book called *Seedlings of the Drought, or, The Collected Shards of J.M.S.*

Give Joe a nice finger fuck for me. I mean, I send my best regards and hope the novel is going well.

And a pat on the ass to you my friend:

Come sempre con amore,

J

PS I assume you haven't sent me your play[51] because you haven't copied it yet. I do every day snatch hopefully at the mail.

PPS Anne came in as I was finishing your letter to Fairfield.

Anne: How's Frank?

Fairfield: Here, you can read it.

---

50. Schuyler refers to Mary McCarthy's (1912–1989) short story "The Man in the Brooks Brothers Shirt"—Porter had painted Schuyler wearing a yellow button-down Brooks Brothers shirt.

51. Perhaps O'Hara's play *The Thirties*, lost when the bag it was in was stolen from a Pennsylvania Station locker.

Anne: Oh, I didn't mean to hint, I just wanted to read the letter.

PPPS If it were imaginable that you might not come, I think Kitty might pull a "Saffo" (off the rocks before the house) with the rest of us Indian file behind her. So you see "you owe it to your public . . ."

Only the advertisement says, "You owe it to your audience," doesn't it. Oh dear—

Waiting for Frank
A Penobscot Bay Play

ANNE: How's Frank?

FAIRFIELD: Here, you can read it.

ANNE: Oh, I didn't mean to hint. I just wanted to read the letter.

KITTY: Daddy is probably the best person on the island. (*Fairfield smiles.*) I love Frank O'Hara; and other men his age. I can just imagine how Frank O'Hara feels about coming here.

JERRY: Kitty, would you please pass me a crumbling slice of bread?

ANNE: I love what Frank says about the Mormons. That they're not healthy. I mean. I mean, that they're not any healthier than anyone else.

JERRY: What's that painting supposed to be? Jimmy Schuyler in a yellow shirt on the porch with a straw hat on the floor beside him and is that pink supposed to be sunlight?

FAIRFIELD: Yes.

JIMMY: It's called, *The Man in the Brooks Brothers Shirt Is Nicer Than Mary McCarthy Said.*

JERRY: I've never read Mary McCarthy. I wouldn't care to.

ANNE: She means well. Furl, do you think they would drink some more coffee if I made some?

ELLEN (*to Jimmy*): Do you think they would?

Jimmy (*to Ellen*): I think they think it's not worth the bother of making it if there isn't any left.

ANNE: I'll make some.

KITTY: Can you imagine Frank O'Hara here? I can.

ELLEN: How is the portrait coming?

FAIRFIELD: Oh it's all right. I haven't spoiled it yet.

ELLEN: I like the sneakers.

FAIRFIELD: So do I. (*He laughs.*)

ANNE: Did whoever was moving their furniture in the middle of the night get it arranged as they like? (*A blank look is passed from face to face until it reaches Jerry.*)

JERRY: It was a boy in fruitless pur-suet of a bat.

(*Enter Jenny. She goes and leans on Anne.*)

ANNE: You've been swimming, Jenny.

FAIRFIELD: Johnny would say you've been spinning, Jenny.

ANNE: Jenny woke me up this morning and looked at me with her big brown eyes. I looked back at her with my big brown eyes. The result was a draw.

KITTY: Perhaps Frank O'Hara will want to go on a picnic.

FAIRFIELD: Anne says she keeps making picnics and then when she goes out she finds peanut butter sandwiches littering the island like leaves.

ANNE: I don't remember saying that.

FAIRFIELD: You said it to Aline last night at seven minutes of seven while we were drinking martinis.

ANNE: I wish Laurence were here. I think boarding schools are a terrible waste.

ELLEN: Why?

ANNE: Because you have these lovely children and then they get the benefit of them.

KITTY: Mother, don't you think Frank O'Hara is a good person? I mean an especially good person.

ANNE: Yes. (*The others laugh.*) I won't have anyone laughing about Frank's goodness.

FRANK: Me either.

KITTY: How did you get here so soon Frank O'Hara?

FRANK: I waded the coast.

ANNE: Wouldn't you like something to eat? You must be tired.

FRANK: No thank you. I'm going swimming—as soon as I beat up Jerry. (*They fall thrashing to the floor.*)

ELLEN: Just like life.

The end.

love,
Jimmy

Beautiful Boy,

I missed the mailboat Monday with my Sunday letter which is just as well as I can now put with it a Monday play. As you'll see, it marks a return to the verismo-metasymbol type play of the post mid-thirties, with an incipient Burglarian resolution. I need scarcely point out to you that Kitty's role is that of the Group Over-Conscious. With that clue, the rest will fall easily into place. (While finding Jung basically anti-pathetic, not to say wrong, I do think we should take what we can of his "useable past," don't you?)

Ho hum.

A note on flight, or tomorrow's travel: F's sister Nancy arrived here by plane yesterday. She flew from somewhere

46

to Bangor, and then took the cutest little red water-landing plane from there here. It looked prettier than Redwing herself when it came out of the sky and landed on the bay. And cost a mere 14.00 (Bangor-Great Spruce Head, of course; I don't know what NY-Bangor fare is). Doubtless you would find it dear, but oh boy it sure beats all for class. (In fact, if I should sell my novel while here, I'd be tempted to return that way with you: the fare for two is 16.50. But how can I dare tempt fate by even thinking about selling my novel? oh oh oh oh oh oh oh oh oh)

I must stop this or I'll miss the mailboat again.

I love you n'uncle.

J

Precious Stone,

Thanx for forwarding mail. I piss in [Henry] Rago's milk, I pooh on his Wheaties. Kenneth's [Koch] letter very funny and cute.[52] There is no missing East Aurora letter. It

52. Henry Rago (1915–1969) was a poet and the editor of *Poetry (Chicago)* from 1955 until his death.

47

must've been one I got a few days earlier than you thought it came. Now rest forever, my tired heart.

My scalp itches. Does that mean I'm going to get money? Or the clap?

I sat for Fairfield again this morning. It's a nice picture but not much of me shows, since it's an *INTERIOR (with figure)*.

Nov. 2nd, 1824, Archdeacon Fisher to John Constable ". . . Abernethy says that there is not a healthy man in London; such is the state of the atmosphere and mode of life . . ."

Now if you would wish to fly—am I not persistent, insistent, a baggage and a bore? But if you should wish to, I quizzed Nancy Porter Straus (Mme. Michel S.) until she thought me a most odd young man; quite queer and pokey. Northeast Airlines arranged EVERYTHING for her. It cost: $30—from LaGuardia to Bangor; $2 from the airport at Bangor to the river and hydroplane; $14.50 for the hydroplane from the Penobscot River to the fluttering white hankies on the dock at Great Spruce Head. Sounds expensive, doesn't it? Well, it is. But oh my liver and lights, if I could have done it instead of busing . . . (the hydroplane, by the way, is called "The Down East Air Taxi Service.")

If worst comes to worst, and it will: you'll see, we can go

48

back by bus together. Two make it more bearable than one, and we can pass the night playing the new game that's the rage of Bahia, feelies.

I think liquor makes a lovely hostess gift don't you? And would you bring me an extra bottle for which I promise to reimburse you? I think vodka is cheap and nourishing.

I haven't been tight once since I left NYC: how long is it since I've gone weeks without some sort of hangover. My nerves are snapping with good health.

The day is so still, the sky so bright, the clouds so fleecy, and silver toned, the spruces so scarcely stirring, the cawing of the crows so distant, the lapse of the tide so gentle, the droning of the fly so freighted with meaning, the air warmed to so faint a fragrance of pitch and grass and salt, I can only sign myself,

your devoted adorer,

Jimmy

ps I started another novel. So far it seems to me rather narrow and mean; a little pinchbeck; repetitious, halting; a bit purblind; not too inspired; somewhat lacking in imagination; rising to sudden and uncalled-for flights of fancy, only to fall as flat as a da Vinci designed plane; perhaps it errs too on the side of insistence, of promising to deliver more goods than its got; nor is its language remarkable for freshness, force or felicity. Its wit is in its feet and its feet are in the mud.

All the same, I think I'll go on with it.

C/O PORTER

48 SOUTH MAIN STREET

SOUTHAMPTON, NEW YORK

OCTOBER 17, 1955

MONDAY EVENING

Dear Frank,

"I love you, you beauteous thing; I seek and adore you."

R. Bridges

It's terrific out here. The wind is going like sixty, all the branches are lashing around and Laurence's room, which I've got this time, is creaking like a cabin on a ship. Heaven.

I was just out collecting kindling in the woods with Larry [Rivers], Joe & Stevie. I said to Stevie, "Frank says to tell you he hasn't forgotten your birthday." S.: "Yeah." Me: "He wants to know what you want for it." Stevie: "A bird." (or rather, "A burd"; or "buhd"). Larry: "Hey!" Stevie: "And a cage. Any kind of bird I don't care. Of course he doesn't have to do it."

Well, kid, there's a pet shop at the corner of 60th and

50

3rd Avenue; and they sell birds very cheap at some Woolworth's.

Long, lanky Kitty Porter seems willing to put up with me as a dismal substitute for yourself. Aline and Betty P[orter] were here for the weekend and went for long walks on beaches together, while Pat played with Kitty and entertained the Sunday diners with riddles: Why did the little moron jump off the Empire State Building? To show his girlfriend he had guts. That one panicked Anne. So Kitty started making up her own Rose Saylavie[53] (sp?) type riddles: Why did the nothing keep doing nothing? Because he had nothing to do. She can really give a gathering tone.

I finally really started working on my book today, thank God. I mean writing the new parts, not just organizing or outlining or anything sappy like that.

I hope you're getting your Fulerbright (sic.) application done. I can't bear to think of you being stuck in that stupid office with those knuckleheads for much longer. As I said, it's not the getting to Europe that matters it's having at least a year off. If you do get one, and go, you'd probably take three months to get settled. But six or nine months or more is a lot of time to have for work. Anyway I hate the idea that

53. Marcel Duchamp's feminine alter ego, Rrose Sélavy.

the best part of your time is spent on things not worth your while; nothing is worth your while except your writing.

All right, I'll shut up.

I can't tell you how I look forward to Friday. It gives the week a *shape*.

Fairfield is barking at the door; we're going walking.

Je t'embrace.

Love,

Jimmy

Love to Joe

APT. 82

333 CENTRAL PARK WEST

NEW YORK CITY

MARCH 27, 1956

Dear Frank,[54]

I've already had breakfast and it's not quite nine yet—an hour with which I haven't the greatest acquaintance (it's really quite a *cute* time of day)—and I'm about to set off on

---

54. O'Hara was in Cambridge, Massachusetts, on a six-month residency at the Poets' Theatre, during which he appeared in John Ashbery's play *The Compromise*. He quickly grew to hate Cambridge and frequently returned to Manhattan.

another round of pleasure: the Parma Gallery, the City Center Gallery... "Hello, this is Mr Schuyler at *Art News*?[55] I said this is Mr. . . ." Ho hum.

This nonsense is only to tell you I love your poems in *Poetry*; as always, in that cutting garden of salmon pink gladioli, they're as fresh as a Norway spruce. Your passion always makes me feel like a cloud the wind detaches (at last) from a mountain so I can finally go sailing over all those valleys with their crazy farms and towns. I always start bouncing up and down in my chair when I read a poem of yours like "Radio," where you seem to say, "I know you won't think this is much of a subject for a poem but I just can't help it: I feel like this," so that in the end you seem to be the only one who knows what the subject for a poem *is*. And I can't think of a word for the lines for James Dean—it's too real not to make "moving and strong" sound very corny.[56] Thank God you at least haven't got a fat eyelid in your beautiful head! (You certainly gave away which is your heart—and homeland—though, when you called G.W. "Dear father of our country" and Rachmaninoff "dearest father of all the Russias." I think they had better replace all those pictures of Stalin with pictures of you.)

55. Schuyler had begun writing reviews for *Art News*.
56. "For James Dean," reprinted in *Meditations in an Emergency*.

Which reminds me: Alvin [Novak] and Kyriena [Siloti][57] are thickening like hollandaise: after his last lesson she started telling him about her flight to Siberia, the supposed death of her father and getting a phone call in China from Rachmaninoff in Belgium, saying he wasn't dead. In the middle of it Alvin started crying so they had lunch together and Kyriena said, "I think you love Russia: shall we go see *Uncle Vanya* together?" Angels, both.

John [Button][58] has been a major resource and joy to me since you and all went away. I can't think what would have become of me without him—I guess I would have spent more time than I do growling at my navel.

I do like the Char poems in your issue of *Poetry*—though I feel—or suspect—that the [Richard] Wilbur translations are tidier than the poems must be—*que pense-tu, b.s.?*[59]

I don't know yet when I'm coming to see you & *The Compromise*. The deadline this month is the fourth; so

57. Alvin Novak, pianist, and Kyriena Siloti (1895–1989), pianist and teacher and daughter of the great Russian conductor.

58. John Button (1929–1982), painter with whom Schuyler fell in love. Button found it impossible to return the feeling.

59. Line from Marcel Carne's film *Les Enfants du Paradis*, "Que pense-tu, beau sphinx?" often quoted by Ashbery, O'Hara, and Schuyler.

after that, Morris [Golde][60] is driving up, and Jane [Frei-licher] & Joe [Hazan] are driving up—but—Besides, I'm feeling a touch bored with Morris. He took me to the ballet a while ago and, my dear, he was quite a drag. I don't like him less than I did, but I kind of feel like slipping him into a cedar chest along with a few pomander balls for a while. (Doubtless this is a prelude to me calling him up and having a very friendly chat!)

Well, the squat dealers are beckoning with their greasy wings; it's time for me to put on my space shoes and Airtex shirt and fly.

Sweet Frank, I love you and miss you all the time. I'll see you sooner than this sounds. Oh Mexico, are you just another dissembling dream? Isn't amoebic dysentery real? Or getting staked out next to an anthill in the warm sun? And the boys diving off the cliffs—surely they exist outside the pages of the *National Geographic*?

Tutt' amore, Francone—

Jimmy

---

60. Morris Golde (1920–2001), businessman and music patron who called himself an "art song junkie." He had a house on Fire Island where O'Hara was staying on the weekend of his fatal accident.

Francey Man,

Thank you for the two letters and the one cheque. I don't know whether I can thank you for the poem, which has embedded itself in my eye; it's upsetting because it's true and therefore beautiful.

What props't, thou ask'st, in these sad times my heart? The shelf of the vanity table on which I keep it stoppered; though it's not a very well fitting stopper, since it hasn't prevented most of the scent from evaporating. It left a gluey residuum in the bottom of the phial, which rather makes a comment on the label: "Joy, The World's Costliest Perfume." My heart is also like: last October's apple; a flowering branch on which the tent caterpillars are at dinner; an empty Three Bromides tube; a Hardoy chair with a shoe in it; a punctured tennis ball; a pocket with 12 cents in it outside the furthest subway stop; Baby Katherine's diapers; the overture to *Lallah Roohk*; a kitchen match without a tip; half a pair of scissors; eight women with one Between the Acts Cigar; a movie review in *Cue*; the unwritten pages from *Death's Jest Book*; a garbage disposal unit logged with cellophane; a self-threading needle; a song from *Inside U.S.A.*; in other words, it's fine and much as you last saw it.

So mine's an angel: the angel part is true but not the part about the "mine." Thank God A. is coming home; I miss him.

"Heart, have you no shame?" "Why? Should I?"

I had dinner with Ken-Jan [Koch] last night. Kenneth has written (natch) a fistful of poems, some of which I loved: particularly one about The Jews and a kind of troubadour ode to St. Catherine of Siena. Janice was studying for a language exam and muttering to herself in Anglo-Saxon about the Great Vowel Shift. She read me a snatch by or about Caedmon, which sounded kind of like [Lotte] Lenya singing the Havana Lied.

(Kenneth got quite cranky when I said I liked *The Tempest* because it's like a Balanchine ballet—)

Speaking of snatches (big greasy ones): so God has tapped Daisy Dildo Face [Aldan][61] for the gift of speech, hey? (Looking at those flayed cheeks I've often wondered if Countess Olga's muff is any softer than a Dutch Maid Copper Scouring Pad)—and when I recall that when the first *Folder* came out I thought she must feel so humiliated

61. Daisy Aldan (b. 1923), a poet and the editor of the poetry magazine *Folder*.

by seeing her poems in print I felt impelled to write her that I liked them! I'd like to sack her apartment and find that note and burn it. Ah well, it's a lesson to us all: pat a fool and you'll get a fang in your flank. But leave her to me—a pound or two of boiling jelly beans up her cooze ought to calm her down a bit.

Kenneth told me that [John] Ciardi[62] sent John's [Ashbery] book to be reviewed for the *Saturday Review* to—Donald Hall.[63] I faint! I fail! I can't walk on these three-inch spike heels! Can you live?

Your Joe [LeSueur], John [Button] and I went to a prevue of Lionel Abel's *Absalom*:[64] my dzear . . . you couldn't even laugh at it. Though there was some suppressed belching in the second act when Absalom said something like: "I grow weary of the human voice . . ." And a perceptible shudder went through a part of the audience when King David said to Jehovah (who was hiding in the flies, I guess): "You made me gay, God." *Pas de tout . . .*

62. John Ciardi (1916–1986), a poet and O'Hara's composition teacher at Harvard. Ciardi was literary editor of the magazine *Saturday Review*.

63. Donald Hall (b. 1928), poet who attended Harvard during O'Hara's years there.

64. Lionel Abel (1911–2001), playwright and teacher. *Absalom* was produced at Herbert Machiz's Artists' Theatre.

Well, most beloved of boys, Addermouth here is going down to his sister Kate Kallman's for a quiet Saturday evening of high thinking. How do you think a couple of martinis will go in a stomach in which a few water biscuits are soaking in a cup of bouillon? Not bad? That's what I think. I hope he'll let me play his *Swan Lake* record.

Give George [Montgomery] my love: I'll see you both at the *soiree de gala* on the 18th. And my love to John Wieners,[65] too. I burn to see you, Frank.

love,

Jimmy

ps Tell George that both Rudi [Burckhardt] and Edwin [Denby][66] liked his photograph enormously—I'm sorry I didn't write him about it, but I've been in the reviewing (ugh) life—J

ps I don't know what to say about which poems you should take out. There aren't any *I* can spare—But if they must go I guess the ones you mention are all right—

---

65. John Wieners (1934–2002), poet. O'Hara met Wieners during his six-month residency in Cambridge.

66. Rudy Burckhardt (1914–1999), photographer, painter, and moviemaker. Edwin Denby (1903–1983), poet and dance critic.

Dearest Frankest,

How ARE you? Yes? No? Well, you can tell me sur le weekend.

The boys flew back last Friday, tired, rather tan and not excessively contented. As Bobby said as soon as they got unpacked, "Now let's sublet the apartments and go some place else." I think it's mostly flying across the ocean and the funny things that happen to the time that made them dizzy; today they seem quite ready to plunge again.

Arthur and I spent all yesterday afternoon hanging the John Button, which looks grand in the sunstruck snowscape of our just painted white living room. It's amazing how little furniture one needs if you have a beautiful painting and a grand piano. That is if you don't mind sitting on the radiator.

I'm writing this mostly to remind you to call the cats at the museum (Porter [McCray] and Grace) when you're here—perhaps Grace Davis has written you already, but, if she hasn't: Alvin had a long talk with her and they long

60

to have you back on what seemed most any terms. Among other things, Grace seemed to think that if you wanted you could probably work freelance, which might be nice? Anyway, it didn't sound as though you'll have to dive in on July 1, so you could make as much of the summer thy own as thou wisht. Have you and George had any inspirations?

Today I'm going to start copying my new-old novel: say a prayer to the Charles River God that my fingers will be fleet, the weather propitious and that Harcourt, Brace[67] will look shiningly on my revisions. (Gerda Gloom of course anticipates the worst, whatever that is.)

Kenneth called up last week to register a long complaint because Yale Younger sent back his mss. (don't know if Wystan ever saw it) and Janice did not get a Fullerbright, although she is an alternate, as John [Ashbery] was. John also had just written him asking if he could have Kenneth's teaching job at Rutgers next year, which Kenneth seems to think he ought to give him. Black spring, where have you hidden the lilacs?

Alvin is going to have his tonsils out, if he can get them uninfected for a while; and John is going to Maine with Fairfield and Jerry [Porter] on June 9, a little inspiration of mine: F. had invited me and Arthur. No comment.

67. Publisher of Schuyler's novel *Alfred and Guinevere*.

Well, sugar, I'll see you Friday: how long will you stay? Give George my love. Dear angel, I miss you. Arthur sends his love to you.

love,
Jimmy

PS I'll have your 50 for you when you come; I've been carefully not cashing my *Art News* check so it will stay intact.

48 S. MAIN

SOUTHAMPTON, NEW YORK

LAST WED. IN JUNE, BLESS US, 1956

Darling Frank,

The enclosed was to have been page one of a letter conceived in the scale of the great *couloir* at Thebes, an inadequate return for your great New Hampshire epistle. Instead, I finished copying m'book, yesterday, to be exact. Of course we all know that Valéry said, that we don't finish a work we abandon it, and old Testy was never righter. Of course I'll keep it by me a day or two and brood on a few significant details—would a woman who is received by the Princess de G but not the Duchess call her backside, "my sit-upon," "my opera box," or just, "tookie"?

Besides, I could scarcely have poured out my heart to you when there's nothing in it but a few drops of *Mouchoir de Mousier* and the stub of an eyebrow pencil. (Actually, finishing the book, though tiring and nerves-making, has put me into a better state of mind than I've been in, in quite a while.)

My social life has been of the least. I've seen John [Button] once, chez lui, with Alvin and Joey, and last night Arthur and I had dinner at KenJan's, with (surprise surprise) Fairfield, who's come down to take the ladies north. He was skunked when we got there and behaved like a fiend but happily became stupefied after dinner when Jane showed up. She's about over her summer cold although she still has a thrilling cough. Baby Katherine [Koch] is so big! And entertaining. I adore her.

I had a cute letter from John [Ashbery], full of malice for John [Bernard Myers] and Herbert [Machiz] and complaining that he hasn't heard from you in 3 months. Tsk tsk. He's going to Italy about July 15 and coming here about Sept. 1; which date it will be before we know it.

Janice got a Fulbright after all, though they haven't decided if she'll accept it.

I'm longing to get to Southampton. We don't quite know yet when we're going, but the pianos are going Monday so I suppose we'll follow soon after.

I'd give my eyeteeth to have seen Maria [Tallchief][68] in the *Dying Swan* with you and John. Lucky boys.

Forgive this prattle. Write me your news, plans, hopes, dreams and ambitions. I miss you dearie dearie.

My love to George and a seductive glance at Mr. Silk.

ever your,

Jimmy

JULY 4

Dear Frank,

Will I ever mail this letter I wonder as my gaze strolls around Fairfield's studio and out the window into the gray beyond? We're here, the pianos are here, my typewriter is here, the grass is green, the ocean cold, I'm on a diet and I'm hungry. But I am thinner. You can't think what I was gettin' to look like sweetie, 'specially stript; though you doubtless noticed but were too kind to call me lardass.

Everything's different but it's all the same. I don't know ...

Write me a dishy letter and I'll write you one that would wring tears out of a stone (if that's your idea of a good time).

68. Maria Tallchief (b. 1925), the first internationally known American ballerina, danced with the New York City Ballet from 1947 to 1965.

I love you I love you I love you I love you I love you I love you and here's a big kiss SMACK. And one for Joey HUG. Take good care of JB [John Button]. I'll see you soon but not soon enough.

love,

Jimmy

48 S. MAIN

SOUTHAMPTON, NEW YORK

JULY 23, 1956

Dear Frank,

Would you turn down my bed, please?

And have you noticed that when my life is troubled it's to you I turn, invariably? I hope you like it and I don't make you feel like an old pillow.

This time I'll *try* to remember not to leave the milk out of the frig.

After some pretty difficult times and a brief chat I told A. [Arthur Gold] I was going to New York—I don't quite know which day yet, soon. We haven't said we're breaking up, though that's what I assume it will turn out to be. Nor did John's [Button] name come into it, nor is there any reason why he should have. From things you said on Larry's [Rivers] lawn that night, I know you're aware of the pressures that would, and did, make for estrangement. To be simple and inexpressive, our egos in a very real way are at cross-purposes—and it's come out more and more in our social lives and in private. I think you understand.

Don't feel anxious that I'm upset: I am, of course; but more than that, I'm certain that it's the only thing to do. And I'm scared, so you'll have to pat your dopey friend and re-assure him that there's more to life than the figure lurking in the doorway. Oh for a nice sandy place that's warm and sunny at Christmas, where the treacherous blue makes an-other delivery of vaporous diamonds each time the waves tick! And a patio with a lizard (a small lizard) asleep under a geranium leaf. And a pair of huaraches you really couldn't wear on the street in New York. Dear Frank, do you think *l'esprit des cartes postales* will devour us? I can hear me screaming in the seventh reel as they drag me toward the anthill, "It was those cursed postcards that brought me to this pass! Open the door, mother, I'm coming."

Are you there, or in New Hamp. or where? I can't get Jane away from the 21 table, which she is out of the rain at, long enough to ask her. Also with her, in no particular order are Arthur, Arthur, Bobby, Larry, Molly, Al K., Nellie, and Joe.[69]

69. Arthur Gold, Arthur Weinstein, Robert Fizdale, Larry Rivers, Molly Adams, Al Kresch, Nell Blaine, and Joe LeSueur.

And as soon as I take this to the P.O. I'll ask to be dealt in, too.

(I hope that doesn't make you feel left out: if we took a popularity vote by secret ballot, you know who would win: *you*.)

No one knows about A and me, at all (though I'm writing John, of course) so . . .

I'll call you or wire or something.

with love, dear,

Jimmy

ps I wrote Vance that I want to review for the Sept. [*Art News*] issue—which I should think would be the week of August 1.

SOUTHAMPTON, NEW YORK

WEDNESDAY

JULY 25, 1956

Dear Frank,

I just got your sweet letter: you are you, which is something better than an angel.

I still don't know when I'll leave here—in fact I tried calling you yesterday to tell you that exciting fact, but you were out, doubtless at an East of Eden festival, perhaps with

John, who was out too. I asked Jane to tell you that I have keys to 326 [East 49th Street] and to apt. 37, so if you go off and I come in all unannounced I will be able to get in. Though it would be dreariness itself not to find you there. I'm counting on that sand and those roses.

The same day I wrote you I wrote to Vance at *Art News* and told him I do want to review; but I haven't heard from him yet. If I don't tomorrow I'll call [Tom] Hess[70]—it's so BORING of the mail not to arrive here before 5 PM.

I am, as we say in the West, keeping. In an ingrown glacial sort of way. Jane and I went out for a hamburger alone the other night and I was going to tell her a little of this and a little of that but I realized that if I did I might cry. So I just sat and stared at her then came home to bed and Mme. de Sévigné (who is sublime). Nerves, nerves, it's all nerves— Oh magic lake! Will you never dry up?

Tell John [Button] I'm sorry I've stopped writing him but I feel too in suspension to be able to; which I'm sure he understands.

Larry, Jimmy Merrill and David Jackson are coming for a drink shortly.[71] And so on!

70. Thomas B. Hess (1920–1978), editor of *Art News*.

71. James Merrill (1926–1995), poet, and his lover of forty years, David Jackson.

I finally wrote a whole new chapter to replace one that I've picked at, hacked at, toyed with and dandled; and I hope I'm out of the woods. The book is disgracefully tiny—but oh well hell—as long as they put it between boards and everybody in America buys it, I should care. Maybe we should tell the Kochsies to look out for a villa large enough to hold three little toddlers as well as themselves; Tuscany may not be sandy but it has got little lizards—and it's handy to the bay where Shelley drowned. And if you feel terribly youthful you can always swim in the Arno along with the BOYS.

Your letter is so sweet—just like you, my candied rose petal.

Now if I can find an envelope in all this motherfucking mess . . .

je t'adore, t'amo, ti baccio—
Jimmy

It seems to me that the reviewing period will have to be next week, so I'll certainly be there by then? Also, if I can get a ride in I'll let that influence me too—the dollars I'll have with me will mostly be a few crumbling sand dollars—Of course I will try to let you know ahead of time when I am coming—

Puss-in-Boots,

The old crank would like to see "in," 3 Penny, Now I am quietly waiting, and There I could Never be a Boy.[72]

Can you really leave out Debussy, which I love?

And there's Les Etiquettes Jaunes, The Stars are tighter (with or without its last stanza, if its last stanza bothers you), and I like Morning very much.

Personally, I like My hearts a-flutter better than the one called Spleen.

And we don't want to be unfair to "He can rest." Do we now? Of course we don't.

Well, give my love to the sky children. We'll have good times talking about all this.

But mercy, don't think the straight bolts you shoot from your crystal bow are tipped with marshmallow! They're unbending yew fletched with eagle feather. (That means, don't

72. Frank O'Hara either sent the manuscript of his book *Meditations in an Emergency* to Schuyler or asked his advice on what poems to include in the book. "The Three-Penny Opera," "Poem" (There I could never be a boy) dedicated to Schuyler, "Les Etiquettes Jaunes," and "Mayakovsky (My heart's aflutter!)" appear in *Meditations*, published by Grove Press in September 1957.

be silly and mistake sincerity and inspiration for sentimentality and goopiness.)

Je t'adore, fils du Baltimore, *mon oriol, oiseaux sauvage!*
Jimmy

PS I fainted twice and then ascended into the sky (just to the left of the UN Building) when I got to the lines in "There I could never" about "as if I were Endymion . . ."

438 EAST EIGHTY-SEVENTH STREET[73]

NEW YORK CITY

JAN. 5, 1957

Dear Curator-en-chef—

Here I am, all tucked up on what I hope is the coldest day of the year with Brahms' 2nd (Serkin, natch) on the phono, and a toasty *roman policier* beside me (D. is out with his boss)—thinking of you & Paris & hoping you're having as much of a ball as weather & art commitments allow.

I really thought I was dying the day you left, of cancer of the vocal tubes, at least. But those anti-biotics David [Pro-

73. Schuyler was living in the apartment of art dealer Donald Droll, with whom he was having an affair.

tetch][74] prescribed worked, though not in time for me to get any more out of New Year's Eve than tucked-in by D, who then rushed off to Hoboken and ministered similarly to Alvin [Novak], whose doctor says she's (she's a woman) seldom seen any thing come out of a sinus quite like what's coming out of his. Bright green . . .

MOMA is unadulterated hell at the moment. I went in on Saturday & drafted some drafts, which wasn't so bad, since it got them off my mind & Porter is cute when he has time to be chatty. But he has Peter working full time (including last Sunday) on the "social functions" for the N.Y. French Drawings, & Peter (& Renee, & Rose, & Sondra) is completely suitified. Miss Woodruff, on the other hand, is in 7th heaven. (I wonder if this is the kind of paper you can write on both sides of? Let's just see—) I know the rich & the great are Vital to our kind of work, but it is maddening when you have to wait till 5:20 to get a cable about something real O.K.'d because who can sit next to whom is being thrashed out.

I just had a chat with Joe, who liked the new Stravinsky less than some, & preferred the Schoenberg. He has blocked off your room (it is incredibly bitter & windy here)

74. David Protetch (1921–1961), college friend of Chester Kallman who became an MD and was Auden's doctor.

and is reasonably snug. He's also being badgered by Herbert, & I seconded your advice, that he should do his play the way he wants to, & to get an agent—In fact, he has talked to Schaffner, who may pass it on to Audrey Wood,[75] which would put him in a very strong position.

I had lunch with Charlotte today, who was in rare good spirits. I think she must be getting it. At least she kept implying she'd been quite wicked on her holiday—

I won't describe what Helen is being like—"re-activated" covers it—

How is Hopping John [Ashbery] and his Pierre [Martory]?[76] You needn't write when you'll be back so soon.

It does seem a shame you boys won't be at Chester & Vera Stravinsky's birthday party on Wednesday. I only wish I could trade places with either of you. Enjoy your self—

love,

Jimmy

75. Audrey Wood (1905–1985), agent who represented Tennessee Williams, among many others, in movies and theater.

76. Pierre Martory (1920–1998), French poet, novelist, and editor.

Dear Frank,

Thank you for your sweet Roman letter. I would have answered it pronto, but I was at Kenneth's and didn't get it until Donald [Droll] came out for Labor Day weekend, when we removed to the Hazans'. Then the absence of a typewriter, the presence of many people, a reading of Arnold's [Weinstein] play *The Red Eye of Love*,[77] all seemed to make writing a letter quite impossible. But then, you have been to the Hamptons. I also heard Kenneth give a reading at the 5 Spot. It is my opinion that the Hamptons were a far, far better place without it.

Bill Weaver and I riotously agreed that it was utter tragedy we weren't there to scour your puss in Rome until you said, "I love it, uncle." I saw Bill at a Welcome Weaver, Farewell [Grace] Hartigan[78] shindig night before last that was quite a little something. Are you aware, chérie, that not only are Jane and Bobby Isaacson pfft, but so are Arthur

77. Arnold Weinstein (b. 1927), playwright. *The Red Eye of Love* had its first production in New York in 1958.
78. Grace Hartigan (b. 1922), painter.

Weinstein and Bobby F. [Fizdale], and that Bobby I. and Arthur W. are living together? When they made their entrance I'm afraid I lurched a little too heartily in the direction of the gin bottle. But there are a few things one really doesn't anticipate . . .

Grace looked chic as all get out; but then, you've probably seen her full many a time by now. Give her a kiss for me.

The International Program is all moved, though scarcely settled, into its new quarters. I'm going to love our new office with its stunning view of one of the Whitney galleries and its 90-foot ceilings, at least I will as soon as a lot of heavy clods quit standing on my desk and playing with the air-conditioning unit, which obviously only needs to be plugged in. Also, every time I confront the mess HMF left me heir to in the French-Drawings-way I wish I had perfected my trans-ocean missile gun. The dear girl also threw a lot of original stuff into a manila folder at the last moment and went scampering off to the airport bus without leaving so much as a list of what she'd taken. So when people like Mrs. Parkinson ask to see things I don't know how long to dig before admitting defeat. Oh well. Waldo [Rassmussen] makes a soothing chief of staff. (It is really quite odd, with you, Porter, Peter, Susan in Europe, Renee away and Cynthia gone. I suppose pretty soon Beth will be organizing the loan shows.)

Mercy, what a grouch I am. But you see, I've also been reviewing. I even have an appointment for 7:30 on Sunday! Some downtown heps, natch, or I wouldn't bother to go . . .

Alvin went to a preview of the Ballets Jerry Robbins and hated it so much he wouldn't go back stage afterward. John Button went to the first night of the City Center and says it was sold out but he was the only person he knew there.

I saw Mike [Goldberg] in the country—he had taken in one plate or color job or whatever you call it for your book, and Richard [Miller] and Floriano[79] were suitably thrilled (have you seen Joan's [Mitchell] and Al's [Leslie]? They're knockouts). I finally batched together about 16 poems and gave them to Grace to take with her; if it's viable, ask to see them, and if you think any should be nixed, please be Frank, Frank.

Well, it's evening, Donald is at a dinner party, I am typing in the middle of a heap of bills and hoping you can have some European time to yourself now that Berlin is all festivaled. I can't wait to hear *all*. What's this about you walking

79. Floriano Vecchi (1921–2005), artist, printer, and publisher.

into a gallery in Rome and meeting someone? Hmmm?
And I can't even remember who told me . . . it *was* a big
party.

   love,

   Patsy Kelly J.[80]

PS Julia Gruen was born September 2nd, weight: 6½
pounds[81]

---

80. Patsy Kelly (1910–1981), Broadway musical star and then a Hollywood comedienne.

81. Daughter of writer, musician, and photographer John Gruen and his wife, painter Jane Wilson.

EPILOGUE

Janice Koch telegrammed the news of Frank O'Hara's death on July 25, 1966, to James Schuyler and Fairfield and Anne Porter on Great Spruce Head Island, Maine. A day or two later, after the *New York Times* obituary had appeared, Schuyler wrote to John Ashbery, "I still feel stunned by the news of Frank's death." Ashbery wrote back with the details Schuyler had requested, and when Janice Koch arrived on the island soon after, she supplied what Schuyler called "a more credible context" for the accident that took O'Hara's life.

A month later Schuyler wrote in passing to Ashbery, "I just had a horrible encounter with a wasp, a glass and a piece of cardboard. I won." This must be the victory with which Schuyler begins his elegy for O'Hara, "Buried at Springs." Perhaps Schuyler's first great poem, its emotional power is in its indirection: O'Hara's early death is not lamented, nor is its effect on Schuyler mentioned. As Schuyler did so frequently, he concentrates on what is right in front of him. Looking out the window in Maine he sees the same view and hears the same sounds O'Hara saw and heard when visiting Great Spruce Head eleven years previously. But nothing is the same, "even the boulder quite / literally is not the same." Somehow life masks this fundamental fact, but death delivers it like a blow. O'Hara is now in all that Schuyler sees and hears. It is "a faintly clammy day / stained by one dead branch / the harsh russet of dried blood." The prolonged harsh *s*'s and blaze of unseasonable color intensify O'Hara's death. Schuyler is stunned, simultaneously fully alive and numb, beyond the reach of grief.

Five years later, in 1971 when O'Hara's *Collected Poems* appeared, Schuyler greeted the book with "To Frank O'Hara." "And now the splendor of your work is here . . . and now people you never met will meet / and talk about your work." Where O'Hara's poems had been written to readers he knew with no public in mind, death intervened to "complete" the work he left famously scattered among a few books and many friends. Poems written for all the occasions an active, passionate life provided are now literature, fitted out with all the apparatus, "even a colophon." Between the lines is the lived world in which a poet who did not pause to organize or promote his poetry wrote these poems.

Schuyler remembers O'Hara's dazzling charm, reckless daring, sexy grace—all attributes of his poetry—and his penchant for staying up all night, his unquenchable flame.

O'Hara's voice is in every line of his poetry. No objective correlative here. His poems have a personality—"even your lines have / a broken nose." What Schuyler most remembers is the fun they had: "The Merry Widow" coming on the radio during O'Hara's attempt to teach Schuyler how to drive, breaking them up. Sophie Tucker, the last of the red-hot mamas, delivers the poem's closing words. Like her "gold tea service," O'Hara's *Collected Poems* is "way out on the nut." (A volume this large, John Ashbery notes in the book's introduction, would have surprised even O'Hara.) The humor O'Hara found in Tucker's words points to a quality in O'Hara's poems much valued by Schuyler. O'Hara took pleasure in life, a fact he did not keep from his work, and as a poet he gave pleasure, more than he could have known.

Schuyler wrote no other poems to his friend. In conversations with the art critic Peter Schjeldahl, who began but never completed a biography of O'Hara, Schuyler gave a full, loving, funny, and astute portrait of his friend. He also spoke for the record to Brad Gooch, whose biography of O'Hara, *City Poet*, appeared in 1993. Others have explored Schuyler and O'Hara's friendship, and, as interest increases in their work and in the New York School of Poets in general, more will do so. Of course, poets who write as well as Schuyler and O'Hara never have the last word. Nor do those readers and writers who never knew them but are now devoted to their work. They all participate in an ongoing conversation, the hum of literature of which these letters are a part.

ACKNOWLEDGMENTS

The Letters of James Schuyler to Frank O'Hara follows *Just the Thing: Selected Letters of James Schuyler*. I hope I have remembered what I learned in editing that book. Thanks again to all those who helped in that effort; this time around I have a shorter list of thank-yous, but the fact remains that to edit this book I needed every bit of help given. Maureen Granville-Smith, Frank O'Hara's sister and executor, yielded these letters so that this book could exist; Darragh Park was, as always, there when called upon, and Trevor Winkfield titled this book. Thanks too to Anne Porter, Ron Padgett, Nathan Kernan, Anne Dunn, and John Ashbery for information and advice. Brad Gooch's *City Poet* and Joe LeSueur's *Digressions on Some Poems by Frank O'Hara* were invaluable.

A special thanks to Michael Gizzi, who, on a gorgeous June day in Vermont, stayed indoors and went over every word in this book, assisting in a number of corrections.

I love the thought of a book this size, a companion easily slipped into a coat pocket for subway-ride or lunch-hour reading. Thanks to Jonathan Rabinowitz of Turtle Point Press for taking it on.

William Corbett (1942–2018) was a poet, essayist, educator, editor, and publisher. He taught at Harvard, MIT, and NYU, and lived in Boston's South End and, later, in Brooklyn. He also edited *Just the Thing: Selected Letters of James Schuyler, 1951–1991,* published by Turtle Point Press.

Printed in the USA
CPSIA information can be obtained
at www.ICGtesting.com
JSHW081704070824
67745JS00002B/11

9 781885 586483